A *Lover's* KEEPSAKE

A DK PUBLISHING BOOK

Created by Amazon Publishing Limited
DESIGN Adrian Morris
PICTURE RESEARCH Veneta Bullen
PHOTOGRAPHY Andrew Kolesnikow, Dave King, DK Studio
ILLUSTRATION Jane Thomson

Dorling Kindersley
MANAGING EDITOR Jemima Dunne
MANAGING ART EDITOR Philip Gilderdale
EDITOR Fergus Collins
SENIOR ART EDITOR Karen Ward
PRODUCTION Patricia Harrington
U.S. EDITOR Lauren Brown

First published in the United States by
DK Publishing, Inc.
95 Madison Avenue, New York 10016

Visit us on the World Wide Web at http://www.dk.com

Copyright © 1997 Dorling Kindersley Limited, London

ISBN 0-7894-1473-2

Color reproduction by
Mullis Morgan Group plc
Printed in Hong Kong by
Wing King Tong

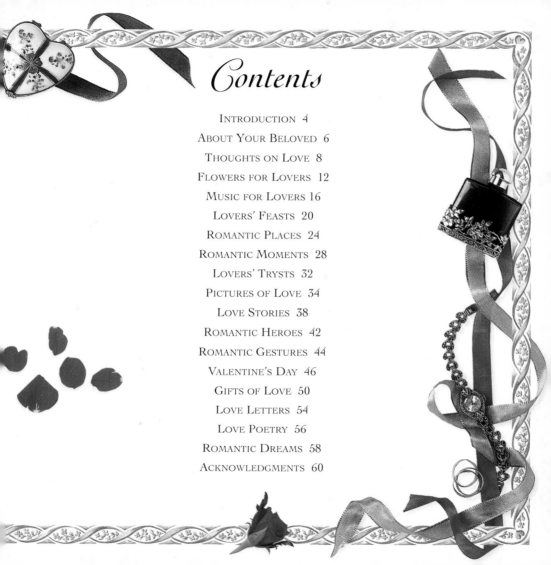

Contents

Introduction 4

About Your Beloved 6

Thoughts on Love 8

Flowers for Lovers 12

Music for Lovers 16

Lovers' Feasts 20

Romantic Places 24

Romantic Moments 28

Lovers' Trysts 32

Pictures of Love 34

Love Stories 38

Romantic Heroes 42

Romantic Gestures 44

Valentine's Day 46

Gifts of Love 50

Love Letters 54

Love Poetry 56

Romantic Dreams 58

Acknowledgments 60

Introduction

Everyone would agree that falling in love is just about the best feeling in the world. Whether your own love story started as a spark that ignited when your eyes met across a crowded room, or was built slowly on solid foundations, you will want to remember the details before they are forgotten in all the excitement. Record your feelings in this book and treasure it for ever as a reminder of how you felt when you fell in love.

About Your Beloved

You're in love. And whatever your lover is like – artist or academic, raven haired or redhead, sports fanatic or computer buff – it seems to you like a match made in heaven. Write down his or her personal details here.

Loves me, loves me not, loves me...

NAME

....

LIVES AT

....

DESCRIPTION

....

WORKS AS

....

FAVORITE HOBBIES

....

WHAT YOU LIKE BEST ABOUT HIM/HER

....

....

PASTE A FAVORITE
PHOTOGRAPH OF YOUR
BELOVED HERE

Thoughts on Love

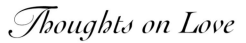

Since time began, men and women have tried to define love. The truth is that everybody's experience of love is unique, but some will strike a particular chord with you. Write down your favorite sayings about love here.

SAYING

....

....

BY, DATE

SAYING

....

....

BY, DATE

....

*Love guides the stars towards
each other.*

Friedrich von Schiller

PHANTASIE AN LAURA

In the past, women used
fans to express feelings of
love to their suitors.

SAYING

....

....

BY, DATE

....

SAYING

....

....

BY, DATE

....

SAYING

....

....

BY, DATE

....

If there was such a thing
as immortality, love
was probably at its heart.
Norman Garbo

Thoughts on Love

*I don't want to live — I want to love first,
and live incidentally ...*

Zelda Fitzgerald LETTER TO F. SCOTT FITZGERALD

SAYING

....

....

BY, DATE

....

SAYING

....

....

BY, DATE

....

SAYING

....

....

BY, DATE

....

*To love is to place our happiness in the
happiness of another.*
Gottfried Wilhelm von Leibniz

10

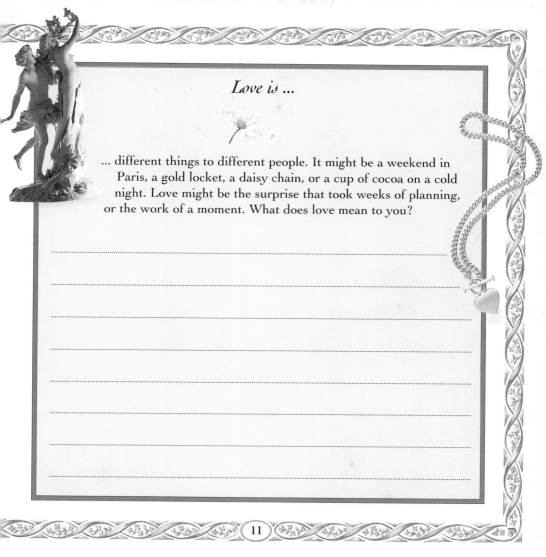

Love is ...

... different things to different people. It might be a weekend in
Paris, a gold locket, a daisy chain, or a cup of cocoa on a cold
night. Love might be the surprise that took weeks of planning,
or the work of a moment. What does love mean to you?

Flowers for Lovers

What better way to say "I love you" than with a
gift of flowers? Whether it is a single white lily
or a dozen red roses, hearts melt at the sight
of a floral offering. Each bloom can be
treasured forever by pressing or drying.

DATE FLOWERS RECEIVED
....

OCCASION
....

BOUQUET INCLUDED
....

....

....

Dear pretty one, do you not see?
Your own sweet fragrance has
bewitched the bee.

Anon

12

Everlasting Flowers

DRY OR PRESS SOME
PETALS FROM YOUR
FAVORITE BOUQUET
AND PASTE THEM HERE

Flowers for Lovers

Did you know that people hide their love,
Like a flower that seems too precious to be picked?

Wu-ti PEOPLE HIDE THEIR LOVE

DATE FLOWERS RECEIVED

....

OCCASION

....

BOUQUET INCLUDED

....

....

DATE FLOWERS SENT

....

OCCASION

....

BOUQUET INCLUDED

....

....

....

Love is a springtime plant that
perfumes everything with hope.

Gustave Flaubert

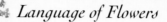

Language of Flowers

Flowers have had symbolic meanings since the earliest times, and you can give almost any message in a bouquet of flowers. Whether you want to offer first awakenings of love (*purple lilac*) or true love (*forget-me-not*), fidelity (*ivy*) or a return of happiness (*lily of the valley*), you can say it with flowers.

Alyssum *Worth beyond beauty*
Amaryllis *Timidity. Pride*
Apple blossom *Temptation*
Aster *I share your sentiments*
Bluebell *Constancy*
Borage *Bluntness*
White camellia *Perfect excellence*
Red chrysanthemum *I love*
White chrysanthemum *Truth*
Jonquil *I desire a return of affection*
White lily *Purity. Sweetness*
Mimosa *Sensitivity*

Myrtle *Love*
Red pinks *Pure love*
Red rose *Love. Beauty*
White rose *I am worthy of you*
Red tulip *Declaration of love*
Water lily *Purity of heart*

Music for Lovers

Music has always had the power to stir the senses and arouse passions. From the beginnings of history, and in every part of the world, it has been used to express love. Whether you prefer Spanish flamenco or the Indian sitar, Cretan flutes or rock and roll, you will almost certainly have a special song, a piece of music that recalls a romantic memory for you.

TITLE

....

ARTIST

....

WHEN AND WHERE YOU HEARD IT

....

....

In medieval France, troubadours serenaded their loved ones with the enchanting tones of the lute.

Music is the imagination of love in sound.

W. J. Turner ORPHEUS

TITLE

....

ARTIST

....

WHEN AND WHERE YOU HEARD IT

....

....

TITLE

....

ARTIST

....

WHEN AND WHERE YOU HEARD IT

....

....

Give me some music; moody food
Of us that trade in love.

William Shakespeare ANTONY AND CLEOPATRA

Music for Lovers

We are the music makers,
We are the dreamers of dreams.

Arthur O'Shaughnessy
<small>WE ARE THE MUSIC MAKERS</small>

TITLE

....

ARTIST

....

WHEN AND WHERE YOU HEARD IT

....

....

TITLE

....

ARTIST

....

WHEN AND WHERE YOU HEARD IT

....

....

O, Love's but a dance
where time plays the fiddle.

Henry Austen Dobson <small>CUPID'S ALLEY</small>

18

Love Lyrics

Sometimes it is the words of a song, rather than the tune, which mean so much when you are in love. Record the lyrics of your favorite love song here.

LYRICS

....

....

....

....

....

TITLE

....

ARTIST

....

Lovers' Feasts

What more romantic way to spend time together than
enjoying a delicious candlelit meal for two? Or perhaps
a picnic by a lake on a hot summer's day? It is hard to
know whether it is love that makes food taste so good,
or good food that makes love thrive.

WHAT WE ATE

....

....

WHERE AND WHEN

....

OCCASION

....

She found me roots of relish sweet,
And honey wild, and manna dew;
And sure in language strange she said,
'I love thee true'.

John Keats LA BELLE DAME SANS MERCI

Love grows cold without food and wine.

Latin proverb

WHAT WE ATE

....

....

WHERE AND WHEN

....

OCCASION

....

Aphrodisiac Foods

Legend has it that certain foods
guarantee a night of passion.
Try these out and see if any of
them work for you!

Oysters   Pomegranate

Lobster   Figs

Avocado   Chocolate

Asparagus   Tomato

Quails' eggs

Ginseng

Honey

Passion Fruit

WHAT WE ATE

....

....

....

WHERE AND WHEN

....

OCCASION

....

....

....

Lovers' Feasts

Love feedeth only upon love.
Italian proverb

WHAT WE ATE

....

....

WHERE AND WHEN

....

OCCASION

....

WHAT WE ATE

....

....

WHERE AND WHEN

....

OCCASION

....

....

The way to my senses is through my heart.
Mary Wollstonecraft Shelley

A Romantic Dinner for Two

Set the table with flowers and napkins, and put on your favorite romantic music. Light the candles, offer a glass of cool, sparkling champagne, and serve as follows:

Pear and Fennel Salad
Slice 2 pears and arrange on plates with thin slices of fennel and celery. Dress with a mustard vinaigrette and garnish with nasturtium flowers.

Chicken with Cranberry Sauce
Pan-fry 2 chicken breasts with 3 halved shallots, and 3 crushed juniper berries. Cook until golden. Add to the pan the juice and finely grated rind of 1 lime, a little chopped tarragon, 2 tsp sugar, 1 cup (100g) cranberries, 4 tbsp chicken stock, and seasoning. Heat until the cranberries begin to pop, and serve with new potatoes.

Figs and Caramelized Grapefruit
Place the shredded, blanched rind and juice of 1 grapefruit in a pan with 2 tbsp sugar and ¼ cup (50ml) water. Cut crosses in 6 figs and add them to the pan. Simmer for 5-10 minutes and serve. Finish with coffee and heart-shaped biscuits.

Romantic Places

The world is full of romantic places, where few can fail to fall in love. Think of Venice, with its gliding gondolas; the gentle babble of a brook on a summer's evening; the romantic skyline of New York City; the clanging of a San Francisco trolley.

PLACE AND DATE

....

REASON FOR TRIP

....

MOST ROMANTIC MEMORY

....

....

....

Italia! oh Italia! thou who hast
The fatal gift of beauty ...
Lord Byron CHILDE HAROLD'S PILGRIMAGE

Let us stay here in this enchanted place
Made beautiful by love's endearing grace!

Ella Wheeler Wilcox LOVE IS ENOUGH

PLACE AND DATE

....

REASON FOR TRIP

....

MOST ROMANTIC MEMORY

....

....

PLACE AND DATE

....

REASON FOR TRIP

....

MOST ROMANTIC MEMORY

....

....

Cruise around New York City harbor at
sunset to see the magical Manhatten skyline
and the Statue of Liberty.

Romantic Places

Who travels for love,
finds a thousand miles only one mile

Japanese proverb

PLACE AND DATE

....

REASON FOR TRIP

....

MOST ROMANTIC MEMORY

....

....

PLACE AND DATE

....

REASON FOR TRIP

....

MOST ROMANTIC MEMORY

....

....

Come live with me and be my love
And I will all the pleasures prove
That hills and valleys, dale and field,
And all the craggy mountains yield!

Christopher Marlowe
THE PASSIONATE SHEPHERD TO HIS LOVE

26

Close to Home

You don't have to travel to fall in love. After all, it doesn't matter where you are – it is who you are with that counts. From a crowded dance floor to a city park, and from a poppy-filled cornfield to a river's bank, true love can transform almost anywhere into paradise. Use this space to remember the places close to home that are special to you and your lover.

Romantic Moments

When you look back over your love affair there will be moments that stand out in your memory. The first meeting, the first kiss, the first time you said "I love you", the anniversary of your first date, Valentine's Day... or maybe even a proposal of marriage!

OCCASION

....

WHEN AND WHERE

....

WHAT WAS SAID

....

HOW YOU FELT

....

....

In the embrace where madness melts in bliss,
And in the convulsive rapture –
Thus does love speak.

Ella Wheeler Wilcox LOVE'S LANGUAGE

How do I love thee? Let me count the ways.
I love thee to the depth and breadth and height
My soul can reach...

Elizabeth Barrett Browning SONNETS FROM THE PORTUGESE

OCCASION

....

WHEN AND WHERE

....

WHAT WAS SAID

....

HOW YOU FELT

....

....

OCCASION

....

WHEN AND WHERE

....

WHAT WAS SAID

....

HOW YOU FELT

....

....

Romantic Moments

*When your face
appeared over my crumpled life
at first I understood
only the poverty of what I have.*

Yevgeny Yevtushenko COLORS

OCCASION

....

WHEN AND WHERE

....

WHAT WAS SAID

....

HOW YOU FELT

....

OCCASION

....

WHEN AND WHERE

....

WHAT WAS SAID

....

HOW YOU FELT

....

*'Remember me' – 'But that I cannot do:
The heart which should remember goes with you.'*

Anon

PASTE YOUR FAVORITE
PHOTOGRAPH OF YOU AS
A COUPLE HERE

Lovers' Trysts

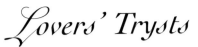

From Antony and Cleopatra to Abelard and Héloise,
secret meetings have always been a vital ingredient
in a passionate love affair, giving extra spice to those
fleeting moments when lovers can be together.

WHEN YOU ARRANGED TO MEET

....

WHERE

....

WHY THE MEETING WAS SECRET

....

....

WHEN YOU ARRANGED TO MEET

....

WHERE

....

WHY THE MEETING WAS SECRET

....

....

Love knows hidden paths.
German proverb

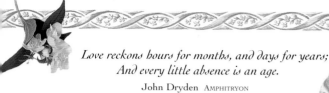

Love reckons hours for months, and days for years;
And every little absence is an age.

John Dryden AMPHITRYON

WHEN YOU ARRANGED TO MEET

....

WHERE

....

WHY THE MEETING WAS SECRET

....

....

Places to Meet

For a romantic rendez-vous
steeped in tradition, arrange an
assignation with your lover at
one of the following:

Barcelona *Las Ramblas*
London *Under the clock at Waterloo Station*
New York *Top of the Empire State Building*
Paris *Musée Jeu de Paume*
Rome *Spanish Steps*
Venice *St Mark's Square*

WHEN YOU ARRANGED TO MEET

....

....

WHERE

....

....

WHY THE MEETING WAS SECRET

....

....

....

....

Pictures of Love

Great artists have always striven to portray the intensity of love in paintings, photographs, or sculpture. From Botticelli's *Venus and Mars* to Gustav Klimt's *The Kiss*, and from Rodin's passionate statues to Doisneau's romantic photographs, their results have inspired lovers through the ages. What are your favorite works of romantic art?

FAVORITE WORK OF ART

....

....

....

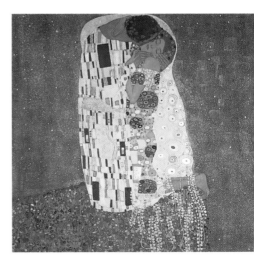

WHEN YOU SAW IT, WITH WHOM

....

....

WHAT YOU LIKED MOST ABOUT IT

....

....

....

Portraits of Passion

Gaze at any of these romantic masterpieces to find echoes of your own great passion.

Scheffer *Paolo and Francesca*
Boucher *Venus and Vulcan*
Sargent *Lady Agnew of Lochnaw*
Maddox-Brown *Romeo and Juliet*
Alma-Tadema *Ask Me No More*
Klimt *Love*
Titian *Bacchus and Ariadne*
Hughs *Amy*
Utamaro *Lovers*

FAVORITE WORK OF ART

....

WHEN YOU SAW IT, WITH WHOM

....

WHAT YOU LIKED MOST ABOUT IT

....

....

Art is the accomplice of love.
Take love away and there is no longer art.
Remy de Gourmont DÉCADENCE

Pictures of Love

*She was a phantom of delight
When first she gleamed upon my sight;
A lovely apparition, sent
To be a moment's ornament.*

William Wordsworth
SHE WAS A PHANTOM OF DELIGHT

FAVORITE WORK OF ART

....

WHEN AND WHERE YOU SAW IT

....

WHAT YOU LIKED MOST ABOUT IT

....

....

....

....

....

....

....

FAVORITE WORK OF ART

....

WHEN AND WHERE YOU SAW IT

....

WHAT YOU LIKED MOST ABOUT IT

....

....

....

FAVORITE WORK OF ART

....

WHEN AND WHERE YOU SAW IT

....

....

WHAT YOU LIKED MOST ABOUT IT

....

....

....

....

Love Stories

Happy or sad, romantic films and plays reflect a lover's deepest hopes and wishes – the desire to find the perfect partner and life long happiness. They echo our own experiences as we search for the fulfillment that only true love can bring. Record here those love stories that have meant the most to you.

MOVIE OR PLAY

....

....

WHEN AND WHERE YOU SAW IT

....

....

WHAT YOU LIKED MOST

....

....

....

....

MOVIE OR PLAY

....

....

WHEN AND WHERE YOU SAW IT

....

....

WHAT YOU LIKED MOST

....

....

....

....

PASTE HERE THE TICKETS
FROM THE MOST ROMANTIC MOVIE
OR PLAY YOU HAVE SEEN

Love Stories

And when Love speaks, the voice of all the gods
Makes heaven drowsy with the harmony.

William Shakespeare Love's Labour's Lost

MOVIE OR PLAY

....

WHEN AND WHERE YOU SAW IT

....

WHAT YOU LIKED MOST

....

....

MOVIE OR PLAY

....

WHEN AND WHERE YOU SAW IT

....

WHAT YOU LIKED MOST

....

....

Words have no language
which can utter the secrets of love.

Hafiz GHAZALS FROM THE DIVAN

A Library of Love

From our first book of fairy tales, we are irresistibly drawn to love stories with happy endings; and the stories of love that have touched us most, can inspire us in our own lives. What books most reflect your own "love story"?

....

....

....

....

....

Love wakes men, once a lifetime each,
They lift their heavy eyes and look,
And lo, what one sweet page can teach.
They read with joy then shut the book.

Coventry Patmore THE ANGEL IN THE HOUSE

Romantic Heroes

From Byron to James Dean, and from Marilyn
Monroe to Greta Garbo, there have always been
individuals who act as a focus for romantic dreams and
fantasies. Who are the personalities you would secretly
most like to have met in a romantic encounter?

YOUR ROMANTIC HERO OR HEROINE

....

WHAT YOU MOST ADMIRE

....

....

YOUR ROMANTIC HERO OR HEROINE

....

WHAT YOU MOST ADMIRE

....

....

Like wind he gallops, like lightning fares,
Can catch the sun or birds in flight.
Dashing across the Central Plain,
How handsome he looks as he glances around!

Hsi K'ang

Illustrious acts high raptures do infuse,
And every conqueror creates a Muse.

Edmund Waller PANEGYRIC TO MY LORD PROTECTOR

YOUR ROMANTIC HERO OR HEROINE

....

WHAT YOU MOST ADMIRE

....

....

YOUR ROMANTIC HERO OR HEROINE

....

WHAT YOU MOST ADMIRE

....

....

....

Romantic Gestures

It is hard to resist a public declaration of love, whether it is by carving your entwined initials on a tree trunk; blazoning a message across the sky; or announcing your love on television. How have you ever publicly expressed your passion for your lover?

ROMANTIC GESTURE

....

....

WHEN AND WHERE

....

ROMANTIC GESTURE

....

....

WHEN AND WHERE

....

'Tis not your saying that you love,
Can ease me of my smart;
Your actions must your words approve,
Or else you break my heart.

Aphra Behn SONG

Emperor Shah Jahan built the
Taj Mahal in India in memory
of his beloved wife.

ROMANTIC GESTURE

....

....

WHEN AND WHERE

....

ROMANTIC GESTURE

....

....

WHEN AND WHERE

....

*I would have had no hesitation,
God knows, in following you,
or going ahead at your bidding,
to the flames of Hell.*

Héloise LETTER TO ABELARD

Valentine's Day

Saint Valentine was a priest and martyr in Roman times. Only centuries later came the tradition of sending romantic verse to a loved one in his name, after Charles, Duke of Orleans, was taken prisoner by the English. From his cell in the Tower of London the Frenchman sent a love poem to his wife on February 14th, 1416.

FAVORITE VALENTINE'S CARD RECEIVED

....

WHO YOU THINK SENT IT

....

MESSAGE

....

....

Wilt thou be mine? Dear love, reply,
Sweet consent, or else deny;
Whisper softly, none shall know,
Wilt thou be mine, love? Ay or no?
Verse from the first Valentine sent by Charles, Duke of Orleans

FAVORITE VALENTINE'S CARD RECEIVED

....

WHO YOU THINK SENT IT

....

MESSAGE

....

....

FAVORITE VALENTINE'S CARD RECEIVED

....

WHO YOU THINK SENT IT

....

MESSAGE

....

....

WRITE YOUR FAVORITE VALENTINE'S VERSE IN THIS SPACE

Valentine's Day

All joy and bliss be ever thine
My idol love, my Valentine.

Anon

FAVORITE VALENTINE'S GIFT RECEIVED

....

WHO YOU THINK SENT IT

....

MESSAGE

....

FAVORITE VALENTINE'S GIFT RECEIVED

....

WHO YOU THINK SENT IT

....

MESSAGE

....

....

To thee, my love,
I give my heart,
I give my love to thee,
Cupid shall ne'er from us depart,
Though thou art far from me.

Anon

Make a Valentine's Card

A hand-made card means much more than one that has been bought, and Valentine's day is the ideal opportunity to spend extra time and attention making something really special for your beloved.

Making a card

Valentine's cards are traditionally square or rectangular, but you can be more adventurous. Try cutting the front of the card into a heart shape – you can use a stencil as a template. Remember to leave a fairly long joining edge on the left hand side, otherwise your card will be too flimsy to stand up. Or you can cut a heart-shaped window into the front of your card. Other intriguing ideas include a concertina-shaped card, or one with two front flaps which open in the middle.

Decorating your card

For the simplest effects, use special papers, such as foils, hand-made papers or tissue papers, in striking shapes and colors. Try reds with blues, bright yellows with greens, or oranges with purples. For a more feminine touch, stick pretty lace or silk onto the card as a background, and then decorate with dried or pressed flowers glued onto the fabric in a heart shape.

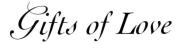

Gifts of Love

A wild flower plucked on a whim from a hedgerow,
or a diamond ring from Tiffany's – it isn't the cost of a
present that counts, but the sentiment behind it.
Love is the greatest gift of all.

GIFT

....

GIVEN BY/TO

....

OCCASION

....

....

GIFT

....

GIVEN BY/TO

....

OCCASION

....

....

*Love's gift cannot be given,
it waits to be accepted.*
Sir Rabindranath Tagore FIREFLIES

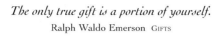

The only true gift is a portion of yourself.
Ralph Waldo Emerson GIFTS

GIFT

....

GIVEN BY/TO

....

OCCASION

....

....
GIFT

....

....

GIVEN BY/TO

....

....

OCCASION

....

....

What can pay love but love?
Mary de la Rivière Manley
THE LOST LOVER

Tokens of Love

Jewels and gemstones have
had symbolic meanings since
ancient times. What messages
has your lover given to you?

Amethyst *Invites the favour of the great*
Diamond *Strength in battle*
Emerald *Riches and fame. Shatters at
marital infidelity*
Garnet *Enthusiasm*
Jacinth *Happy disposition*
Ruby *Love and happiness. Peace and serenity*
Sapphire *Heavenly bliss. Faithfulness*
Turquoise *Prevents accidents*

Gifts of Love

Gift exchanges make love last longer.
Swedish proverb

GIFT

....

GIVEN BY/TO

....

OCCASION

....

GIFT

....

GIVEN BY/TO

....

OCCASION

....

GIFT

....

GIVEN BY/TO

....

OCCASION

....

*To get the full value of joy you must
have someone to divide it with.*
Mark Twain

Romantic Wrappings

You can make any gift romantic by using loving care and
imagination in the wrapping.

Gift boxes

The best way to make even the smallest gift look special is to put it in a box. These
come in all shapes and sizes, from heart-shapes to pyramids, and in all sorts of
materials, from card to precious china. Some boxes are so pretty they need no
further decoration, but thoughtful wrapping adds a very personal touch to a gift.

Wrapping paper

Tissue paper is one of the most romantic of wrappings – use thin, gauzy sheets of
different colours to create a shimmering, translucent effect. Or make your own
wrapping paper by simply stamping or stencilling hearts, cupids, doves, or your
lover's initials onto plain wrapping paper. If you like découpage, wrap the present
first and then stick the cut-out images – from gift wrap or magazines – onto the
finished item. Don't forget to make a matching heart-shaped gift tag!

Ribbons and bows

Ribbon is available in a huge variety of colors, patterns, widths, and fabrics,
and by curling the ends (just pull the ribbon along an edge) you can
create the ultimate in romantic wrapping.

Love Letters

Few things are as highly valued as a love letter. Those words, written in the heat of the moment, or labored over to communicate the intensity of passion, can be treasured for ever. They can be read again and again for pleasure and reassurance, and passed on to future generations as a reminder that love is truly timeless.

YOUR FAVORITE LINES FROM A LOVE LETTER RECEIVED

....

....

....

WRITTEN BY, AND WHEN

....

....

....

*It's like begging for mercy of a storm
or killing Beauty or growing old, without you.*
Zelda Fitzgerald to F. Scott Fitzgerald

I am not writing to you, no, I am close beside you.
I see you, I hear you.

Franz Liszt to Marie D'Agoult

YOUR FAVORITE LINES FROM A LOVE LETTER RECEIVED

....

....

....

WRITTEN BY, AND WHEN

....

YOUR FAVORITE LINES FROM A LOVE LETTER RECEIVED

....

....

....

WRITTEN BY, AND WHEN

....

....

And oft, the pangs of absence to remove
By letters, soft interpreters of love.

Matthew Prior HENRY AND EMMA

55

Love Poetry

Perhaps it is poetry that expresses love best.
Nothing sways the heart so much as the lines of a poem,
revealing a lover's innermost feelings. Write down here
the verses of romantic poetry that mean the most to you.

TITLE OF POEM AND AUTHOR

....

YOUR FAVORITE LINES

....

....

TITLE OF POEM AND AUTHOR

....

YOUR FAVORITE LINES

....

....

....

....

This heart-shaped manuscript
belonged to a troubadour, who used it to
record his sweet music and verses of love.

TITLE OF POEM AND AUTHOR

....

YOUR FAVORITE LINES

....

....

....

TITLE OF POEM AND AUTHOR

....

YOUR FAVORITE LINES

....

....

....

TITLE OF POEM AND AUTHOR

....

YOUR FAVORITE LINES

....

....

....

*Poetry is the record of the best and happiest
moments of the happiest and best minds.*
Percy Bysshe Shelley A DEFENCE OF POETRY

Romantic Dreams

Falling in love is a phenomenon that no one can explain. But it is sensational when it happens, like freefalling through space or treading on air. No wonder then, that most people want it to last for ever, to enjoy a fairytale romance. What are your romantic dreams for the future?

....

....

....

....

....

Like the ice which melts
When spring begins
Not leaving a trace behind,
May your heart melt towards me!

Anon

Do you want me to tell you something really subversive?
Love is everything it's cracked up to be.
That's why people are so cynical about it.

Erica Jong HOW TO SAVE YOUR OWN LIFE

Alter? When the hills do.
Falter? When the sun
Question if his glory
Be the perfect one.

Emily Dickinson
ALTER? WHEN THE HILLS DO

Acknowledgments

Dorling Kindersley would like to thank Malcolm Hillier for the recipes on page 23, first published in his book Good Food Fast. Amazon Publishing would like to thank Jane Packer Flowers Ltd for the floral heart on the cover and Wilson Design Associates for typesetting.

Picture credits

t=top, b=bottom, m=middle, l=left, r=right

Advertising Archives: 32br; Bridgeman Art Library: 8r Lauros-Giraudon, 10bl Wallace Collection London, 34r Osterreichisches Galerie Vienna, 37br Giraudon; e. t. archive: 8l, 9tr, 27br, 28bl, 35br, 36bl, 36tr, 37tl, 38bl, 55tr, 55br; Fine Art Photographic Library: 29tr, 32bl, 18tr; Mary Evans Picture Library: 30r, 44br, 45tl, 57br; Portfolio Pictures: 56b; Retna Pictures: 19tl, 19tr; The Ronald Grant Archive: 39t, 39bl, 40tr, 40b, 42bl, 43tr, 43b; Zefa Pictures: 24r, 25tr, 26br, 29br, 30bl, 33r, 45br, 58bl.

... loves me